Essential Question
How do people make government work?

The Race *for the* Presidency

by **Mary Atkinson**

Introduction

If you have ever voted for a class president, you probably know that students choose between two or more classmates. These are the candidates. In order to convince people to vote for them, the candidates create posters and give speeches in which they promise to make positive contributions to the class. On election day, everyone votes for the candidate who has impressed them the most. The candidate with the most votes wins the election.

Kelly Ca, a 12th grade class president in Philadelphia, introduced President Obama when he gave his Back to School speech in 2010.

The elections for the president of the United States are similar to class elections, but the process is longer and there are many more steps.

Presidential elections are held every four years. The race for the presidency begins more than a year before the election. The candidates have a lot to do before Election Day.

To run for president, a candidate must be eligible. They must follow the rules set out in the United States Constitution.

WHO CAN BE PRESIDENT?

The Constitution has only three rules about who can be president. It states that a president must:

★ be at least 35 years old

★ be a natural born U.S. citizen

★ have lived in the U.S. for 14 or more years

Theodore Roosevelt was the youngest president. He was 42 when he took the Oath of Office in 1901.

3

Chapter 1

The Primary Campaign

The race for the presidency begins with the **primary elections**. Most of the candidates who run for president are members of a political party. This is a group of people with similar ideas on how to run the country. In the United States, the two main parties are the Democrats and the Republicans. In primary elections, the voters in a state decide which candidate from each party will go on to the general election.

A candidate can also be **independent** or run for a smaller party. Independent candidates do not belong to a party. They must gather their own supporters.

THE TWO MAIN PARTIES

The Democratic Party has been active since at least 1828. It aims to bring equal opportunities and justice to all people, whatever their status or wealth.

★ Anti-slavery activists started the Republican Party in 1854. Today, the party aims to protect individuals' rights.

Each state organizes its own primary elections. The first state to hold a primary is usually New Hampshire. This primary gets a great deal of press coverage, and all the candidates want to win. The New Hampshire primary can make or break a candidate.

Some states schedule their primaries together on a Tuesday in February or early March. This day is known as Super Tuesday.

A few states don't hold primary elections. Instead, the parties choose their candidates at a special meeting called a **caucus**. A caucus is a closed or private event run by a political party. It is open to all registered voters belonging to the party.

2008 Democratic candidate Hillary Clinton talks to the public outside a polling place during the New Hampshire primary.

5

During the primary season, presidential candidates try to get as much media coverage as possible. They want to convince people to vote for them. They take every opportunity to be interviewed and photographed. They give speeches, meet with voters, and attend public events. They explain their policies and outline what they will do if they become president.

The voters learn about the candidates and their positions on issues by reading newspapers and watching TV. Then they decide whom to vote for.

Voters go to a polling place to cast their vote.

After the primaries, the two main parties each hold a national **convention** to finalize the selection of their presidential candidate. **Delegates** from each state attend the convention and represent their state in an overall vote. A candidate must gain a majority of the votes to be selected. Each party then announces its candidate for president. The presidential candidate also announces who will run for vice president on the same ticket.

When the candidates have been chosen, it is a time for speeches and celebrations. It is also a time for the parties to discuss the policies they will put forward in their **campaign**.

Balloons and confetti dropped onto the crowd after the candidates for president and vice president were announced at the 2008 Republican National Convention.

Chapter 2

The General Election

After the conventions, the Republican candidate and the Democratic candidate begin their campaigns to become president of the United States. The candidates give speeches and interviews and travel around the country to meet with voters.

Each party works hard to gain support for its candidate. Staff and volunteers plan events and raise money. They run a media campaign that includes everything from posters, stickers, and flyers to sophisticated television advertisements. They run voter education and voter registration programs to encourage people to vote.

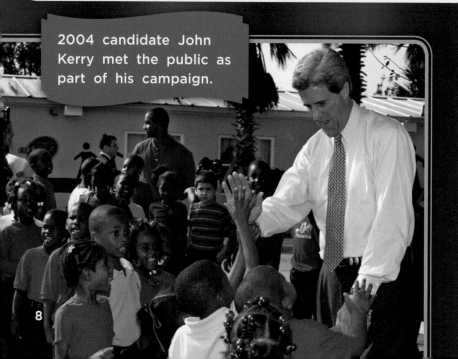

2004 candidate John Kerry met the public as part of his campaign.

To have a chance of winning the election, a candidate needs to know what matters to the public. There are many ways to find out what kind of government people want. Candidates and their support staff talk to people across the country and gather reactions to the campaign. They conduct research to find out what issues are important to voters. They set up opinion polls to find out what voters are thinking. The results of polls may cause them to make changes to their campaign strategy or change the message they deliver in speeches.

CAMPAIGNS IN THE PAST

Candidates in the past couldn't zip across the country in planes or advertise on television. Instead, they used other means to attract publicity. Cross-country train journeys, known as whistle-stop tours, were popular.

Candidates make many campaign promises. These promises focus on the positive actions they will take if they are elected. Voters want to know that if they elect a candidate, the candidate can deliver on their promises. They want to know whether the candidates understand the details of their policies. Reporters from newspapers or television ask the candidates tough questions. They point out inconsistencies and examine the details of the policies. Sometimes voters seek more information by phoning or writing in with questions that concern them.

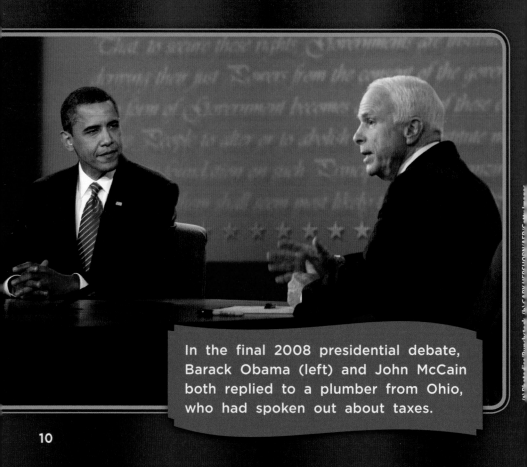

In the final 2008 presidential debate, Barack Obama (left) and John McCain both replied to a plumber from Ohio, who had spoken out about taxes.

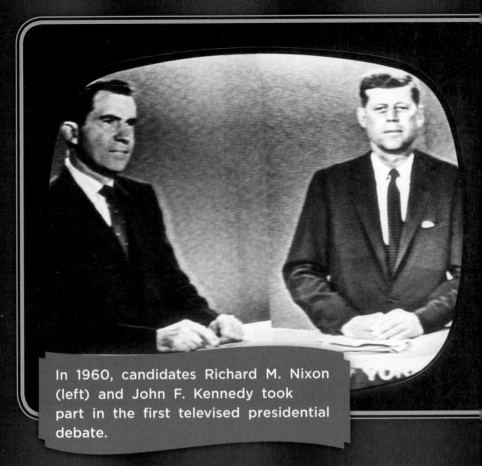

In 1960, candidates Richard M. Nixon (left) and John F. Kennedy took part in the first televised presidential debate.

Televised **debates** are popular ways for voters to find out more about the candidates in an election. Debates focus on how the candidates respond to the issues of the day. When the candidates for president meet in a TV debate, they point out possible problems and mistakes in each other's policies while defending their own policies from attack. The candidates for vice president debate each other, too. These debates can be exciting viewing, but most importantly, they help voters make a decision about how to vote.

11

Election Day

Election day takes place on the first Tuesday after the first Monday in November. This is the day that voters place their votes for president and vice president. People who are old enough to vote and have followed the rules for voting in their state can vote. In most states this means that voters need to be registered. Polling places are set up throughout the country. Poll workers help voters and make sure the elections run fairly.

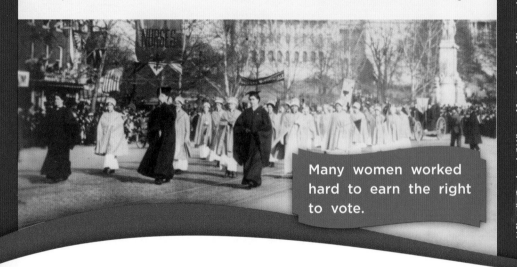

Many women worked hard to earn the right to vote.

VOTING TIME LINE

1856	1870
All white men over the age of 21 have the right to vote.	The 15th Amendment to the Constitution grants African American men age 21 or older the right to vote.

Election day is exciting because nobody can predict the results. Television networks follow the process closely. They show the results for each state and estimate the final vote. Maps indicate which states gain a Democratic win and which gain a Republican win. The tension builds as viewers watch groups of party members celebrating or looking disappointed. Finally the overall winners are announced, but the results are not yet official. A group of voters called the Electoral College must cast their votes for the president. They officially select the president and vice president of the United States.

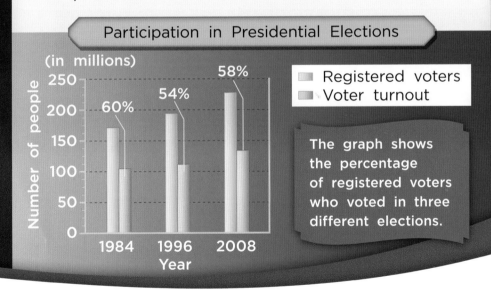

Participation in Presidential Elections

(in millions)

Number of people

60%   54%   58%

250
200
150
100
50
0

1984   1996   2008
Year

■ Registered voters
■ Voter turnout

The graph shows the percentage of registered voters who voted in three different elections.

1920	Today
The 19th Amendment to the Constitution grants women age 21 or older the right to vote.	Most U.S. citizens age 18 or older have voting rights.

It is usually on January 20 that the newly elected president is sworn in. This day is known as Inauguration Day. The ceremony is usually held at the U.S. Capitol in Washington, D.C. Thousands attend, and millions more watch on TV. The Chief Justice of the United States leads the new or reelected president in saying the Oath of Office. The president's term in office has begun.

After the president has been sworn in, he takes part in the Inaugural Parade. The president and vice president lead the parade down Pennsylvania Avenue to the White House.

On January 20, 2009, Barack Obama took the Oath of Office to become the 44th President of the United States.

THE OATH OF OFFICE

I do solemnly swear (or affirm) that I will faithfully execute the office of President of the United States, and will to the best of my ability, preserve, protect, and defend the Constitution of the United States.

Summarize

Use details from *The Race for the Presidency* to summarize the selection. Your graphic organizer may help you.

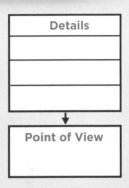

Details

↓

Point of View

Text Evidence

1. How do you know *The Race for the Presidency* is expository text? GENRE

2. What point of view do you think the author has about election day? AUTHOR'S POINT OF VIEW

3. What is the meaning of the word *reelected* on page 14? Look at the prefix to help you figure out the meaning. PREFIXES

4. Why does the author think it is important for candidates to debate each other? Check page 11 to help you with your answer. WRITE ABOUT READING

Compare Texts

Read how students worked with state government to change a law.

Elementary School Lawmakers

In April 2006, a group of nervous third- and fourth-graders gathered in the New Hampshire Senate. These students from Wells Memorial Elementary School in Harrisville wanted to change the law. They wanted to make the pumpkin the official state fruit. The students had found out that pumpkins grew throughout the state. Many had been to the state's annual pumpkin festival.

Every October the people of Keene, New Hampshire, hold a pumpkin festival, with thousands of jack-o'-lanterns on display.

Franz-Marc Frei/CORBIS

16

Harrisville state representative Peter Allen had been impressed with the students' research. He had submitted a bill to the House of Representatives requesting that the pumpkin become the state fruit. At a committee meeting in January, the students had spoken in support of their idea. They had discussed how pumpkins were popular and that tourists would buy pumpkin T-shirts and other souvenirs.

The class had asked other students across New Hampshire to send in postcards supporting the bill. Then, in March, their bill had passed the House vote. The final step to changing the law was for the bill to pass the Senate vote.

VEGETABLE OR FRUIT?

Are pumpkins fruits or vegetables? Cooks and grocers call them vegetables, but scientists call them fruits. This is because, scientifically speaking, a fruit is the part of the plant with seeds. A vegetable is any other part of a plant that we eat. Pumpkins contain pumpkin seeds, so they are fruits. Tomatoes and peppers are also fruits that are called vegetables.

Senator Robert Boyce was an opponent of the bill. He wanted the strawberry to be the state fruit. The students prepared themselves for disappointment. They were unsure which way the vote would go. Finally, the senators voted. They voted twenty-three to one in favor of the pumpkin. It was a victory for the students. They had become lawmakers.

NEW HAMPSHIRE LAW

CHAPTER 3: STATE EMBLEMS, FLAG, ETC.

Section 3:24 State Fruit.

3:24 State Fruit. – The pumpkin is hereby designated as the official state fruit of New Hampshire.

Make Connections

When people vote for a bill, do they know what the result will be? What does this tell you about how governments work?

ESSENTIAL QUESTION

What do presidential candidates do to get people to vote for them? Did the students do the same things to get people to vote for the pumpkin? What did they do differently, if anything?

TEXT TO TEXT

Glossary

campaign *(kam-PAYN)* a set of activities organized to achieve a particular result *(page 7)*

caucus *(KAW-kus)* a closed meeting where a political party chooses candidates or policies *(page 5)*

convention *(kon-VEN-shuhn)* a large meeting held by political parties to choose election candidates *(page 7)*

debates *(duh-BAYTS)* organized discussions between people *(page 11)*

delegates *(DEL-uh-gits)* official representatives to a convention *(page 7)*

independent *(in-duh-PEN-duhnt)* a person who does not belong to any political party *(page 4)*

primary elections *(PRIGH-me-ree i-LEK-shunz)* elections in which party members or voters choose candidates for an election *(page 4)*

Index

Focus on Social Studies

Purpose To see how surveys can be used for campaigning.

What to Do

Step 1 Survey your classmates on a topic of your choice, for example, colors, animals, or fruit. Make a list of six or seven colors (or animals, fruit, or some other item of your choice). Ask each person to tell you their favorite item.

Step 2 Write up the results of your survey. Write the number of people that chose each item.

Step 3 Create a "Vote for..." campaign for the second most popular item. Make a poster.

Step 4 Have a vote between the most popular and the second most popular items.

Conclusion What did you learn about campaigning? Which item did you think would be the most popular? How did the results of the survey change your ideas?